GRAMPY AND ME

*Dec. 2017
To a Special Boy ♥
Happy Reading!
God Bless You —
Suzanne Holko*

SUZANNE L. HOLKO

Copyright © 2012 Suzanne L. Holko.

All rights reserved. No part of this book may be used or reproduced by any means, graphic, electronic, or mechanical, including photocopying, recording, taping or by any information storage retrieval system without the written permission of the publisher except in the case of brief quotations embodied in critical articles and reviews.

ISBN: 978-1-4624-0080-5 (sc)

Inspiring Voices books may be ordered through booksellers or by contacting:

Inspiring Voices
1663 Liberty Drive
Bloomington, IN 47403
www.inspiringvoices.com
1-(866) 697-5313

Because of the dynamic nature of the Internet, any web addresses or links contained in this book may have changed since publication and may no longer be valid. The views expressed in this work are solely those of the author and do not necessarily reflect the views of the publisher, and the publisher hereby disclaims any responsibility for them.

Printed in the United States of America

Inspiring Voices rev. date: 3/08/2012

*To my dear daughter, Kelly, with love (YATWBMW);
in loving memory of my father, Walter, my mother,
Ruth and our neighbor "Grampy" Art.*

All morning Emily kept rushing to her bedroom window. She was waiting for the familiar blue truck to pull into the driveway next door. At last, there it was! Her Grampy was home.

Emily loved to do things with her Grampy. Actually, he was not her real grandfather, but she felt so close to him. The two of them had so much fun together. It was not long before Emily had "adopted" him and the name of "Grampy" fit him perfectly.

Grampy loved surprises. Emily went out to her garden to pick a pretty bunch of flowers to surprise him with. She took great care in picking just the right ones for this special bouquet. Emily could hardly wait to bring them next door!

"Hi, Grampy," said Emily with delight. She reached up to give him the bouquet. "These are for you. I picked them all by myself!"

Her Grampy was indeed surprised! He reached out for the flowers with a big smile on his face. "Oh, thank you, Emily. These are lovely," he said.

Emily gave a big smile back. She was so happy!

When the flowers had been put in water, Emily and Grampy were off to the garden to check the corn. Grampy was very careful, and guided Emily as they walked through the field. He made sure neither one of them tripped on the stubs left from the cutting of the corn stalks.

Grampy explained to Emily that after the rows of fresh corn had been picked, the stalks were pulled together in bunches to form a corn stack. The stacks would gradually turn brown, and would then be cleared away to help prepare the field for the next growing season.

At last they were at the very corner of the field. Grampy showed Emily an ear of corn that looked ready to be picked. They both pushed down together, and the ear of corn broke off the stalk.

There were so many kinds of corn, and Emily was just beginning to learn.

Pulling back the husk, Grampy now showed Emily the corn inside. She touched it and moved her fingers along the bumpy kernels.

This would be the last corn crop of the season.

"Now we will go and see how the pumpkins are doing, okay, Emily?" said Grampy. And off they went to the pumpkin patch!

Emily did not know what to think as Grampy gently pushed aside the green vines in the pumpkin patch. She stared at what was the biggest pumpkin she ever did see, especially growing near her own back yard!

"This pumpkin will be yours come Halloween," Grampy said. Emily could not wait to bring it home to be her very own. It would be so special, and it was the biggest one in the whole pumpkin patch!

Emily had gone to bring her ear of corn home, and to share the news about her special pumpkin. She was soon back again, along with her cowboy hat. Grampy always wore a hat of some kind, and Emily liked that. Today she wanted to be like him.

"Wait for me, Grampy!" Emily shouted, as she came back into the garden.

Grampy was standing there waiting by his tractor. He smiled when he saw her hat.

Before Emily knew it, she was sitting on Grampy's tractor with him. She had always been curious about the tractor. Emily was also a bit frightened by it, because it was so big. Grampy was very careful, and held onto Emily as he began showing her parts of the tractor. Soon Emily was overcome with excitement, and not scared at all!

"When I get bigger, maybe I can ride on the tractor," Emily said. Grampy smiled and nodded his head.

"Let's go and see how the watermelons are doing, Emily," he said. "I think they should be just about ripe, and maybe we can pick one."

The words were hardly out of Grampy's mouth, when Emily had scrambled off the tractor and was off to check the watermelons. She had not gone very far when she jumped back.

"Here is one, Grampy, over here!" Emily shouted.

She could see Grampy shaking his head. It was too small and would not be ready for a month or more. So, Emily went on to check the round watermelons that seemed to be growing faster.

"Oh, look over here, Grampy. Come see this one!" yelled Emily with delight. She was so excited! "This one must be ripe. Come and see it, Grampy!"

Grampy came and knelt down beside the watermelon with Emily. He showed her how to tell if it was ready to be picked or not.

"Knock on it like this, Emily," he said. He took her arm and showed Emily how to test the watermelon by tapping it with her fist. It was hard to describe the sound it made, but after checking it over, Grampy said it was ready to be picked.

"Hooray!" shouted Emily.

"Careful, this is a heavy one, Emily," Grampy said, as he lifted up the watermelon to carry it home. It was all so exciting!

Emily thought again of her pumpkin, and now a watermelon, too! What a fun day this had been. Such fun was found in the garden, from the corn to the watermelons! What would Grampy think of next?

A few days later Emily was back in the garden with Grampy. This time it was to pick potatoes that were already dug up, and to fill bucket after bucket with them.

First, Grampy showed Emily how to look for bad spots on the potatoes. She checked her very first potato and it was fine.

Grampy could not believe how eager Emily was to learn, and what a good helper she was!

Now, the picking began. Grampy and Emily moved up the long row, checking the potatoes as they went. They worked together, and in just a couple of minutes, the bucket was half full!

As Emily put the potatoes in the bucket, she began counting them one-by-one. She soon lost count.

"Oh, Grampy, there are too many potatoes for me to count!" said Emily.

Grampy gave a little laugh. Then he watched as she put the potatoes in so carefully. It was time for a new bucket.

Emily eagerly began to fill the next bucket.

"You are doing a very nice job, Emily. Some of these potatoes will be yours to take home, because you are such a good helper," said Grampy.

Emily smiled and kept right on working. Oh, how she loved to help her Grampy!

As the morning went on, Emily began to get a little tired. She held onto the special hoe that Grampy had given her, and watched as he finished digging up the row ahead.

She could remember when they first planted the potatoes. Now, like so many other things in the garden, they were ready!

It had been so exciting to see the first sign of growth in the garden. Although Emily only understood a small part of it, she found it fascinating!

The time had come, and Emily decided to take a rest while Grampy got another bucket to fill. She sat down among the potatoes and began to sort them out. One pile was for good potatoes, and one for potatoes with spots.

What a big day it was to help Grampy with the potatoes. So much to learn, and so many buckets to fill!

As summer was soon coming to a close, there was also work to be done in the yard. The next afternoon found Emily and Grampy raking up the trimmings from a bush.

"I like helping you, Grampy," Emily said.

"And I like having you as my helper, Emily," Grampy replied, as he gathered up the trimmings.

Then they thought they spotted a caterpillar in the leaves. Emily moved her special blue rake to see. She was disappointed. It was just a dried up leaf, but it looked so alive!

Grampy and Emily continued to work together cleaning up the trimmings in his yard.

"When I get this big," Emily said, as she put her hand up to her head, "I will be like you, Grampy, and a bigger helper, too!"

Grampy kind of smiled and laughed at the same time. He nodded his head saying, "I bet you will be, Emily."

"I'll tell you what we can do after we finish up here, Emily," said Grampy. He gathered up the last pile of trimmings. "We can share a watermelon that is just your size, okay?"

"Okay!" Emily squealed with delight. She hurried to finish, and knelt down to help pick up the pile.

This would be the first watermelon Emily had ever tasted fresh from the garden. She had even helped Grampy plant the seeds!.

A few minutes later, Grampy and Emily were seated on his front porch with the watermelon cut and ready to eat.

"Here you are, Emily. To my biggest and best helper," Grampy said. Emily reached out and took her piece of watermelon.

"Thank you, Grampy!" said Emily, with a happy smile.

The watermelon smelled so good! They both began to eat, and neither Emily nor Grampy stopped to talk. It was so delicious!

Emily and Grampy found the watermelon to be so very refreshing after working in the yard. They began to get silly and laughed and giggled.

Emily did not know what to do with the pits. She tried putting them in her hand, but they fell onto the steps. Some of them stuck to her pants!

"You are funny," Emily said as she looked at Grampy. Then they both let out a big laugh, and giggled until their sides ached.

What a great day!

The next day Grampy had a surprise for Emily. The ponies from down the street had come up for a visit. He was going to take her to see them. They were very gentle. Grampy had brought a carrot along so Emily could feed them.

He watched very carefully as Emily fed the carrot to Ginger. Ginger was quick to take a bite, as Smokey looked on waiting for his piece of the carrot.

Emily loved the ponies, and she was so excited when Grampy put her up on Smokey's back! It was a very special time when the ponies came for a visit.

"Make sure you hold onto the mane, Emily," Grampy said. That is just what she did. What fun!

When they had finished their visit with Ginger and Smokey, Emily and Grampy decided to go for a walk. As they passed by the stacks of corn stalks, Emily found herself sitting upon one. She thought it was great fun and began to laugh.

"Look at me way up here, Grampy!" Emily yelled. "See how big I am?"

Grampy gave another one of his laughing smiles to Emily. Then he helped her get down.

Down the road they went for their walk, after another day of sharing. These would always be special times Grampy and Emily spent together.

"You are fun, Grampy!" Emily said with a giggle, and took his hand.

Emily held tight onto her Grampy's hand and, without a word, they said "I love you."

CPSIA information can be obtained
at www.ICGtesting.com
Printed in the USA
LVIW010113300512
283780LV00001B